GREAT BARRIER REEF

By Charles Higgins and Regina Higgins

CELEBRATION PRESS

Pearson Learning Group

Contents

Captain Cook and the Coral Reef

In June 1770, Captain James Cook's ship *Endeavour* hugged the coastline of Australia. Cook and his crew had set sail from England in 1768 to explore the South Pacific and, especially, Australia. At that time, Europeans knew little about the Australian continent. Its eastern coast had been mostly unexplored. This is where the *Endeavour* sailed.

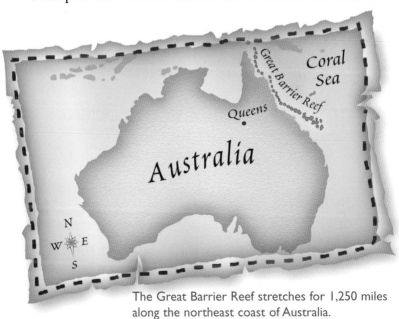

The Great Barrier Reef stretches for 1,250 miles along the northeast coast of Australia.

3

One night, the moon lit up the sky. Cook suddenly saw that the *Endeavour* had sailed into danger. The ship was passing between the land and a long, sharp **coral reef**.

At any moment, the ship could crash into the reef and sink. Earlier, the men had spotted sharks swimming in these waters. If the ship sank, the crew would have to swim to the mainland. The sharks would likely attack them.

Everyone worked silently. They moved the ship slowly and carefully through the water. Finally, they thought they were out of danger.

Cook believed the ship was safe. He was relieved but very tired. So he went to sleep in his cabin. All of a sudden, a loud crash awoke him. He rushed on deck to see what had happened.

The *Endeavour* had hit the reef. Now the ship was caught on the coral. Seawater poured into the ship. Waves pounded the *Endeavour* against the reef. Cook gave orders to his crew. They began to throw overboard whatever they could to lighten the ship.

Captain James Cook

The Great Barrier Reef nearly sank Captain James Cook's ship, the *Endeavour*.

Water was still pouring into the ship, so the crew used pumps to keep the ship from sinking. Finally, the rising water from the tide lifted the ship off the reef.

While water continued to leak into the ship, Captain Cook guided it into a nearby harbor. There, the crew began the difficult job of repairing the ship's hull, or body.

As they worked, the crew found a large chunk of coral stuck in the ship. The coral had acted like a plug and slowed the water coming in. Imagine everyone's surprise when they found out what had happened. Although the coral reef had nearly sunk the *Endeavour*, it had also saved the ship from sinking.

Since Captain Cook's time, people have learned more about the sea and the reef where Cook's ship nearly sank. Scientists have explored the reef, mapped it, and even given it a name.

The reef that Cook's ship struck is now called the Great Barrier Reef. It's not really one solid reef, but many separate reefs. They stretch for about 1,250 miles along the northeast coast of Australia.

Scientists believe the reef started forming about 500,000 years ago. That is a long time, but the reef is still young compared with some coral reefs.

How the Reef Grows

The Great Barrier Reef is *great* because it is so big. It's so big because it has been growing for such a long time.

The Great Barrier Reef is actually the largest coral reef in the world. It measures about 135,000 square miles, which is bigger than the state of Nevada. The reef is so large that astronauts can even see it from space.

From an airplane, people can see how big the Great Barrier Reef is.

Tiny coral polyps built this reef.

In fact, the Great Barrier Reef is the largest structure on Earth built by living creatures. The creatures that helped build the reef over thousands of years are called **polyps** (PAWL ihps). Most of these tiny water animals measure less than an inch across. Some are almost too small to be seen. Most polyps are about the size of an eraser on the end of a pencil.

At the beginning of its life, a soft baby polyp attaches itself to the reef. Then it absorbs, or takes in **calcium carbonate**, or limestone, which is a mineral in seawater.

The calcium carbonate helps the polyp to grow a hard outer shell. The shell protects the soft polyp when it is closed. When the polyp is open, it uses its tentacles to catch food.

All its life, a polyp remains connected to the reef. The coral polyp feeds on zooplankton, which are tiny animals that float in the water. Single-celled **algae** (AL jee) live inside a polyp's body. The algae use sunlight to make food for themselves and for the polyp.

After it dies, the polyp's skeleton remains connected to the reef. New baby polyps fasten themselves onto the skeletons of dead polyps. Then the process begins again.

When you look at a reef, you're seeing the skeletons of thousands of generations of polyps. Over time, a special kind of algae called coralline algae fills in holes between the polyps. The algae deposits calcium carbonate that acts like cement. Then, over time, the waves smooth the rough surface of the reef.

This process repeats itself over and over again. So, as long as baby polyps continue to attach themselves to the reef, the reef will keep growing.

The Living World of the Reef

Imagine diving into the waters of the Great Barrier Reef. What living things might you see among the coral? The reef contains more varieties of plants and animals than you might find in the same size area anywhere else in the world. Some animals here are small, like worms. Other animals can be large, like sharks and dugongs. Dugongs are also called sea cows.

The tiger shark hunts for fish, turtles, sea birds, and even other sharks.

Sharks in the reef are usually just curious rather than dangerous. However, the possibility that sharks were in the water must have troubled the *Endeavour*'s crew so long ago. The sailors might have seen bronze whalers, gray reef sharks, or silvertips, which are 5 to 10 feet long. There may have even been tiger sharks 20 feet long among the coral.

Anyone who dives into the waters of the reef would need to watch out for big creatures like these sharks. Divers might also look for large animals such as sea turtles and dugongs.

The Great Barrier Reef is an important nesting area for sea turtles. Six of the seven **species** of sea turtles live in the reef, as well as in the waters of the Great Barrier region.

Dugongs are mammals. They grow up to 10 feet in length and weigh about 800 pounds. They eat plants. Dugongs are endangered, meaning there are only a few alive today. Most of the world's remaining dugongs live in the Great Barrier Reef.

Divers could watch for smaller creatures living here, as well. There are about 350 kinds of reef-building coral and some 4,000 different varieties of **mollusks**. These sea animals usually have hard shells to protect their soft bodies.

One of the most common types of coral in the reef is called staghorn coral. The name describes the shape of the coral. It reminds some people of a deer's antlers.

Staghorn coral is a great reef builder.

Other kinds of coral also have names that describe what the coral looks like. Brain coral looks like a large brain. It is rounded with many twisting, ridges in which the polyps live.

Another kind of life in the reef is the sea cucumber. This animal looks like a large pickle. However, most are brown, black, or bright yellow instead of green. Sea cucumbers attach themselves to rocks or move along the sea floor with two rows of tube feet. The feet have tiny suction cups on the ends.

There are many sea stars on the reef, too. They are also called starfish. Most people think sea stars have five arms, but they can have many more. When they lose one of their arms, they grow another one.

There are almost 2,000 kinds of fish in the Great Barrier Reef. People discover new kinds every year. Some fish are named for land animals they look like. A brightly colored parrot fish has large teeth at the front of its mouth that remind most people of a parrot's beak.

The large black dot on the butterfly's tail looks like an eye.
Predators think the tail is the fish's head.

Butterfly fish were named for their bright scales that are colored like a butterfly's wings. There are many varieties of butterfly fish.

Some scientists believe the reef fish are so colorful because there are so many kinds of fish there. Colors may help a fish to recognize another of its kind in these crowded waters. Patterns may help fish blend into the background to escape being eaten. Whatever the reason, the reef is a beautiful living world!

The Reef's Ecosystem

As you have seen, many different kinds of life grow in and around the thousands of reefs that make up the Great Barrier Reef. In fact, the reef forms its own **ecosystem**.

This ecosystem includes the many plants and animals that live together in the underwater world around the reef. It also includes all of the plants and animals that live on the islands that have formed above the reef.

There are more than 600 islands around the Great Barrier Reef. Some of the smaller islands, called **cays**, formed when soil and pieces of coral skeletons and shells in the seawater collected on top of the reefs. Many of the cays are bare sand without any vegetation. Some cays have plants and trees, such as seagrass and palms, growing on them. Since the cays are far from the coast, you may wonder how these plants got there.

A black noddy traveled to a reef cay with a seed stuck to its feathers.

Over the years, sea birds have stopped to rest on the cays. They drop seeds from fruits and plants they have eaten. These seeds take root in the soil and grow into plants and trees. Then the plants attract more birds to the cays to feed.

Under the water, the ecosystem has expanded, too, thanks to the Great Barrier Reef. The reef provides a safe place for sea life, protected from stormy seas.

Within the reef's ecosystem, many creatures form a **food chain**. The very smallest animals and plants are food for the coral polyps and little fish. The little fish are food for slightly bigger fish, and so on. The largest fish swim in during high tide to feed on the smaller fish they find in the reef.

As a result, each part of the reef's ecosystem depends on the other parts. For example, the bumphead parrot fish eats large amounts of coral, but this is not harmful to the reef. It is helpful because the parrot fish eats the algae on the outside of the coral that would otherwise smother the coral.

The coral that the parrot fish does not use for its food is left behind as waste. This waste is pinkish coral sand. The sand builds up and becomes part of the reef and its beaches.

Some plants and animals on the reef need one another to live. This relationship is called **symbiosis**. For example, coral polyps and algae help feed each other.

Algae live inside the body of the polyp and make food for both of them. The polyp provides a home in shallow water where the algae can get the sunlight it needs to make food.

The clown fish and the sea anemone also have a special relationship. Most animals on the reef avoid the sea anemone because of its poisonous stingers.

The clown fish and the sea anemone are partners in reef life.

The clown fish, however, lives right in the middle of the stinging cells in the sea anemone's tentacles. Why don't the stingers hurt the clown fish? Scientists believe that a special skin coating may protect the clown fish from the poisonous stingers. This works well for the clown fish. In the sea anemone's tentacles, the clown fish is safe from bigger fish and can catch smaller fish.

This relationship also works out well for the sea anemone. When the clown fish swims around its tentacles, the sand and algae are brushed off the sea anemone, keeping it clean.

The Great Barrier Reef's ecosystem has grown slowly over thousands of years. Each part, as you have seen, depends on the other parts. For the reef to survive, each part needs to stay in balance with the other parts. When this balance breaks down, however, the reef itself can be in great danger.

The Future of the Reef

The Great Barrier Reef took hundreds of thousands of years to form, but human activities could destroy it in a much shorter time. For example, many tourists visit the reef to see the variety of life there. However, too many people swimming or boating around the reef could damage the coral and harm the ecosystem.

Walking on the reef can break and kill the coral.

The crown-of-thorns sea star is a growing danger to the
Great Barrier Reef.

Another possible threat is the companies that
want to drill for oil around the reef. Because
drilling could endanger the reef, the Australian
government does not allow oil drilling in this
area.

There's also a natural threat to the reef. The
crown-of-thorns sea star, which feeds on coral
polyps, is growing in numbers. Scientists have
been studying this sea animal to find out why
this is happening.

If the crown-of-thorns sea star eats too much of the live coral, the reef could stop growing. Scientists hope to find ways to keep these two creatures in balance.

Many Australians and **conservationists** all over the world are helping the Great Barrier Reef stay alive. The Australian government started the Great Barrier Reef Marine Park Authority to protect this treasure. The United Nations has also made the reef a World Heritage Site. It is important to keep protecting the reef and the animals that live there.

You can help save a part of our world, too. Learn about the Great Barrier Reef. Find out about the dangers that could harm it. Look for news about the reef in the newspaper or on the Internet. Tell friends what you have learned. Your voice along with many others may help keep the Great Barrier Reef alive and growing for many years.

Glossary

algae a plantlike form of sea life also found in fresh water and damp places

calcium carbonate a mineral in seawater used by a coral polyp to create a hard, limestone skeleton

cays low islands made of sand or coral

conservationists people concerned with protecting the environment from pollution and overuse

coral reef an underwater structure created by coral polyps

ecosystem community of plants and animals living together

food chain the sequence or order of how a community of organisms feeds itself

mollusks sea animals with a soft body and usually a hard shell

polyps (coral polyps) small, soft sea animals that attach themselves to coral reefs

species a grouping of plants or animals that are thought to be very closely related

symbiosis two unlike plants or animals living together to help each other survive